DEAR BOOBS

DEAR BOOBS

A book of poems about
the love, leaks and
let-downs of breastfeeding

by Claire Foskett

ABOUT THIS BOOK

The process of making, ejecting and raising a child has been riddled with surprises for me. However many books I read and however much the antenatal classes told me, in the early days I often found myself thinking 'Is this normal?!'. Then I'd look online and see that hundreds of other women had been through the same thing. I loved breastfeeding but I wasn't prepared for all the added extras – the leaking, the restrictions, the sheer relentless monotony of it all. I felt like a bit more of a preview into what to expect might have made those frazzled, foggy times a little clearer.

And that is why I wrote these poems. If you're an expectant mum, I hope they give you a head start and an honest insight into what to expect. If you've started breastfeeding, I hope they reassure you that other women have been through the same challenges.

This isn't a how-to book and it doesn't provide any advice or solutions. I'm not a qualified breastfeeding professional, I'm simply a woman who volunteered her boobs for service for a year and wanted to talk about it.

CONTENTS

For Nora and Avril,
whose persistent demands were the
inspiration for these poems

THE ELUSIVE LATCH

When you and your baby are skin-to-skin,
It's time to try popping the nipple in.
Ready, set, go: Let breastfeeding commence!
Or not. 'What happened to 'the rooting sense'?'

And the elusive latch may take all night.
'It shouldn't hurt if you're doing it right'.
And then comes the suction, the pain, some blood.
'This hurts a lot more than I thought it would!'

'Power on!' they'll tell you, 'Try not to stop!
That colostrum is gold – premium, top!
Breast is best; don't turn to a bottle yet.
Stick with it; it will get better, I bet!'

Milk ducts might get blocked; mastitis might hit.
And they'll still tell you that you should not quit.
Lanolin cream will become your best friend,
Soothing those red and raw nipples no end.

WHEN
BREAST
IS
BEST

Breastfeeding is free –
You'll be glad of it,
As your income's going to take a hit!

Breastfeeding is near –
No need to prepare.
Just whip out your boobs and dinner is there!

Breastfeeding is good –
With antibodies,
To help keep away the cough and the sneeze.

Breastfeeding is great –
Helps weight go away,
Burning hundreds of calories a day!

Breastfeeding is love –
So much time spent close,
Cuddling and bonding with ev-e-ry dose.

EVERYTHING HAS CHANGED

Stretched from pregnancy.

Traumatised by labour.

Exhausted from breastfeeding.

Body and mind will never be the same.

AFTERPAINS

Labour over, contractions done?

Sorry love, there is more to come!

With each feed that you give your mite,

You'll feel your tummy getting tight.

It's just your womb getting downsized;

A few days more to minimise.

'Morning boobs' are of normal size
And hormones much the same
But 'evening boobs' are compromised
And hormones go insane.

Your milk's come in! And with it comes
Some very busy glands
The milk supply of brand-new mums
Needs time to match demands.

The hormone crash might make this day
A hard one to endure
But somehow you will find a way
To come through this – and more.

HOW MANY, HOW MUCH?

Hi Mummy, feed me – on demand; now!
All day, all night – yes, you'll feel like a cow.
Remember the words of that nice lady:
'You can't overfeed a breastfed baby!'

Make sure you give me as much as I need,
I might ask 12 times a day for a feed!
In the evenings I might feed even more,
This 'cluster feeding' can feel like a chore.

Sometimes I'll have one boob, sometimes two.
And other times just a top-up will do.
Sometimes it's not calories that I crave,
But a comfort feed to make me behave.

Some feeds will be done in five minutes flat,
Some will take 20 – or longer than that.
It's the hind-milk I need to fill me up,
Until I'm ready for another sup.

↻

Who knows how much I'm really ingesting,
You could spend days or months second-guessing.
If weight goes up, there are lots of nappies,
You can assume that I'm pretty happy!

So get hold of the things that you might think
You'll need nearby – phone, TV remote, drink.
Get them nearby before you get started,
So once we start we won't need to be parted.

Hi Mummy, feed me – on demand; now!
All day, all night – yes, you'll feel like a cow.
So sit yourself down and set yourself up,
And bring a muslin – in case I throw up.

BURPING

At 4am when nothing's working
My partner says 'Have you tried burping?'
'Of course I've tried burping!' I explode
(I'm already in 'high tension' mode).

Whoever said breastfed babies do
Not get gas – well it is just not true!
Is this it, what my life has become:
Forcing the air out of someone's bum?!

Rubbing and patting desperately
Over my shoulder and on my knee
Pushing the knees and cycling the legs
Still no sleep – is it time for the meds?

Which meds to try – maybe gripe water?
Is it safe for my tiny daughter?
When, how, how much – a spoon or a drop?
How long until the desired pop?

Just as I'm giving up tearfully
Baby's face scrunches and – could it be?
At last we hear the desired release
And finally get a moment's peace.

WHAT A
LOAD
OF IT

Stuff that's like tar
Meconium

Yellow with seeds
Breastfeeding mum

Exploding out
Needs lots of wipes

Often stains clothes
Front, back and sides

After each feed
At first, then less

Could be just farts
Try the 'sniff test'

Fills up your day
Makes you forget

That poo talk is
Poor etiquette

MY LEAKING'S AT A PEAK

I've been trying not to leak
But my leaking's at a peak
All I need to do is speak
About baby and they seep.

It seems dry I cannot keep
Even when I am asleep
When I hear a baby weep
Look at photos of pipsqueak.

Feed from one, the other...eek!
Bathe in water hot and deep
Then the tingle starts to creep
And my leaking's at a peak.

TIRED

Tired.

From pregnancy.

Tired.

From labour.

Tired.

From recovering from labour.

Tired.

From feeding on demand.

Tired.

From broken sleep.

Tired.

From not knowing when it will get better.

Tired.

MASTITIS

Chills, aches and fever

And feeling yuck

Plus red lumpy boob

Where milk is stuck.

But such sweet relief

As baby sucks

And milk flows freely

Through unblocked ducts.

RECIPE FOR BREASTFEEDING MUMS

Ingredients

A block of blue cheese
And a piece of rare steak
And pâté on toast
Full of vitamin A

A small glass of wine
And another coffee
And anything else
Stopped by pregnancy

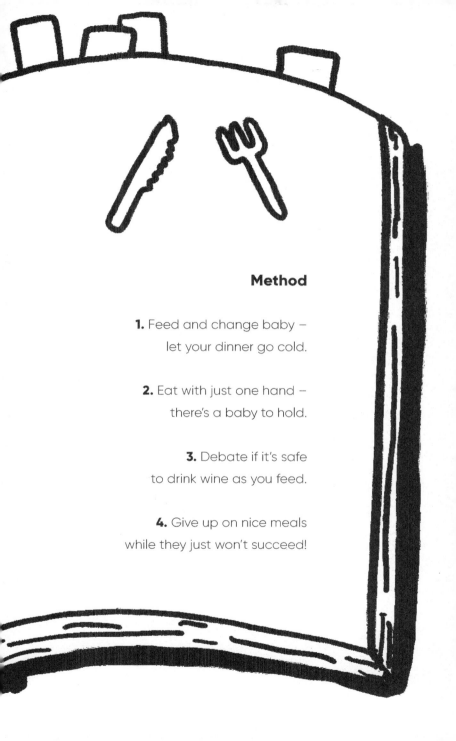

Method

1. Feed and change baby –
let your dinner go cold.

2. Eat with just one hand –
there's a baby to hold.

3. Debate if it's safe
to drink wine as you feed.

4. Give up on nice meals
while they just won't succeed!

TO
THE
LADY
ON
TABLE
THREE

To the lady on table three
Who seems offended by this feed
I'm sorry that you look so fussed
But baby wins so feed I must.

I know you're eating – so was I
Before this thing began to cry
I'll try and do it secretly
With minimal exposure – see?

This baby isn't going to wait
And hold on 'til a later date
It's not that she's a little brat
It's just she wants to have a snack.

This is my only trip today
Outside the house to keep me sane
Please don't make me feel self-conscious
This feeding thing is hard enough!

DEAR
BOOBS

Dear boobs,

What's new?

You're looking different.

Much bigger.

Much fuller.

Much bigger nipples.

I've seen a lot of you recently.

In magic bras with drop-down cups.

But not in long dresses; too impractical.

But not in grey tops; don't want to risk a leak.

But not in see-through tops; don't want my

breast pads to show.

↶

I haven't been out socialising recently.

What's changed?

I haven't gotten used to feeding in public.

I haven't got a babysitter.

I haven't had enough sleep to want to go out.

I haven't been well.

But it isn't about me anymore.

Some medication is off limits.

Too much caffeine is off limits.

Too much alcohol is off limits.

See you soon – for the next feed.

Love from Me x

FLASHING

There once was a lady called Me

Whose right boob hung out – all to see!

The postman surprised

Averted his eyes

And she popped it in hurriedly!

PERIODS - FULL STOP.

No exclamation 'I've come on!'

No dash to get sanitary supplies

No dot dot dots in your knickers

No periods – period.

Periods – full stop.

THE
BREAST
PUMP

A breast pump might not sound much fun:

A noisy whirring contraption

That sucks milk out until you're done

Then swap! Sucks from the other one!

But...

If it's a night off that you need

Or to release some milk at speed

A boozy drink? Then do take heed

Pump, pump away to get that feed!

RELENTLESS MONOTONY

Breastfeeding sounds like it should be magic,

But can, at times, feel way more tragic.

Pump on one boob and baby on t'other –

'This is what it's REALLY like to be a mother!'

SEX?
NO
THANKS!

We could, but....

What if I don't want to?

I don't.

What if I'm too tired?

I am.

What if it hurts?

It does.

What if my boobs leak?

They do.

What if I look different?

I do.

What if she wakes up?

She might.

What if I still love you

But it's different... just for now?

It is.

Sex?

No thanks. Just for now.

A
CAUTIONARY
TALE

Like Cinderella out too late
A mum can also meet her fate
If she ignores the warning signs
And doesn't leave the pub on time.

And so I'll tell you of a tale
That's quite revolting to regale
I'm not sure if it's true or not
But once it's heard it's not forgot.

The story starts (or so I'm told)
In an establishment in Mold
With a young mum on a night out
With japes and larks and pints of stout.

She'd planned to catch the ten-o-four
That dropped her outside of her door
And got her home with time to spare
To pump and dump and wash her hair.

↶

But drinks went down and time did pass
And every drink was not her last
Meanwhile her boobs were filling up
And stretching out her bra C-cup.

'Twas then she felt a little queer
At first she blamed the pint of beer
But soon it was apparent that
The problem was up top in fact.

It seemed protection had been breached
The threshold had indeed been reached
Her bra could no more take the strain
There was no space to stay contained...

Her breasts exploded everywhere
In one man's drink; another's hair
'Punters look out!' the barman cried
As nipples flew right past their eyes.

A milky mess came raining down
As did her bra and coat and gown
'Well what a waste of thirty quid!'
She thought as her bra e-rup-ted.

She needed now an exit plan
She grabbed her things and (drink in hand)
Said 'Sorry' to the barman who
Was cleaning up the beer-milk goo.

And that is why breastfeeding mums
Should always finish off their rums
And make sure they get home in time
Not far too late – like in this rhyme.

DISTRACTED

It's no longer hurting,

They're no longer squirting,

Now baby's decided...

'Oo, int'resting curtain!'

WHAT DOES IT ALL WEAN?

Solids – can't wait to start!

Breastfeeding – can't wait to stop!

Solids – when do I start?

Breastfeeding – when do I stop?

Solids – how do I start?

Breastfeeding – how do I stop?

Solids – just once a day?

Breastfeeding – still five times a day?!

Solids – has he eaten enough?

Breastfeeding – hasn't he eaten enough?!

Solids – now will you sleep through the night?

Breastfeeding – now why won't you
sleep through the night?!

Solids – so much mess!

Breastfeeding – so much less mess!

Solids – how have I got time for this?!

Breastfeeding – bring back breastfeeding!

TEETH

Teeth that pushed through

With a fight.

Teeth that kept you

Up all night.

Teeth so cute oh

What a sight.

Teeth so painful

When they bite!

THE
LAST
FEED

The end of milk feeds.

Independence beginning.

Growing up too fast.

THE
REALITY
OF
BREASTFEEDING

Breastfeeding:

Best feeding.

Best feeling.

But also a bit of a pain.

THANK YOU, YOU, MR. YOUTUBE

(A.K.A. THE MAN'S PERSPECTIVE)

by My Husband

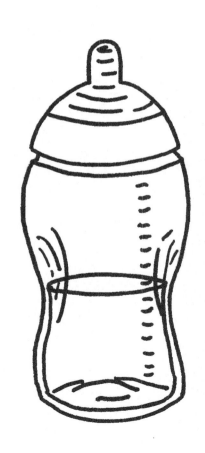

Here I am – the gushing father
Now learn just what she needs.
A new adventure this is rather –
I want to do some feeds.

Being useless is a fear.
I know I should not curse,
As instinct makes her disappear
Beneath a shroud to nurse.

In the night when she has cried,
Does she think I turn my back?
No wicker lays at my bedside
I haven't got the knack.

I am assured the day will come
I hold on to the promise
She won't forever turn to Mum
In need of milky solace.

At four o'clock a hungry yelp
The third one of the night.
Again awake but of no help,
I just switch on the light.

I go through summer and the fall,
Uselessness a concern.
But then one Sunday get the call,
To show that I can learn.

When you do not have a boob,
A bottle you must dangle.
A sharing dad on the YouTube
Shared with me the best angle.

I am trusted in the living room,
Babe, me and Tommy Tipp.
Mummy's fed her since the womb,
Now from me PLEASE take a sip.

I'm grateful wife has gone elsewhere,
It helps me keep my calm.
With pressure off and just us there,
A milk test on my arm.

I take the bottle past 'er eyes,
They are beautiful and blue.
I think you're drinking then realise
Upon the teat you chew.

I change the angle of approach,
And for an hour's quarter,
Recall my friend the YouTube coach
To help me feed my daughter.

It happened pretty slow at first,
The moment that I savoured.
Where at last I quenched her thirst,
And the tiny larynx wavered.

In the doorway gentle cheer,
My wife watched on with pride.
My cheek rolled with a gentle tear,
As all but baby cried.

Laying there with content calm,
My little ginger pup.
Satisfied to use my arm,
To be cradled for a sup.

Dads at first who don't succeed,
And feeding's going bad,
Patience please and just take heed:
The time will come for Dad.

ABOUT THE AUTHOR

Claire Foskett is an ordinary mum who had a pretty ordinary breastfeeding journey (though she didn't know it at the time). A lover of words, Claire is a medical writer, a chatterbox and a keen reader.

Her husband Daniel is delighted to be on the receiving end of her motherhood 'insights'. He is even more delighted that their daughter Nora talks almost as much as her mum.